IMAGES
of England

ERDINGTON

IMAGES
of England

ERDINGTON

Compiled by
Marian Baxter and Peter Drake

TEMPUS

First published 1995, reprinted 1999 and 2001
Copyright © Marian Baxter and Peter Drake, 1995

Tempus Publishing Limited
The Mill, Brimscombe Port,
Stroud, Gloucestershire, GL5 2QG

ISBN 0 7524 0345 1

Typesetting and origination by
Tempus Publishing Limited
Printed in Great Britain by
Midway Clark Printing, Wiltshire

Contents

Introduction

This first ever publication of photographs of one of Birmingham's best known suburbs depicts over one hundred years of Erdington's history. The photographs have all been chosen from the collection in the Local Studies and History section of Birmingham Central Library.

Situated towards the northern limits of the city, Erdington borders on the traditionally affluent and spacious districts of Sutton Coldfield and Castle Bromwich while closer to the city its neighbours are the more working class areas of Aston and Perry Barr. Erdington, though, retains an identity of its own much of which is appealingly captured in this collection of over two hundred photographs.

One of the most striking features of Erdington's past hundred years has been its growth. For example, there are now more pensioners living in Erdington than the entire population in the district in 1891. With this expansion has come a completely changed way of life. An Erdington resident recalling the area in the last century described a village with 'no fire station, no street lamps, no library, no police station. One bank sufficed for its needs and a child could safely play marbles or trundle a hoop in the middle of High Street.' The population was then just over 9,000, and that was a four-fold rise since 1851 when Erdington possessed the grand total of 442 houses.

The extension of the railway from Aston through Erdington to Sutton Coldfield and the ever increasing drift of town dwellers from Birmingham was already changing what had been a straggling agricultural hamlet. The early photographs shown here capture this early rural life which was already vanishing rapidly. Its loss was already being mourned by the 1890s. The isolated farms and cottages interspersed with the manor houses would after this time only survive as photographic images.

Much of the interest of this type of photographic anthology comes from spotting how much is recognizable today - how much has survived and how much has been lost. With Erdington it is a mixed story. Of the large manor houses and grounds which dominated the district, Erdington Hall, Pipe Hall and Wood End Hall have all gone, but Pypes Hayes Hall and park and Rookery House are still with us. The oldest public house, the Lad in the Lane, better known as The Old Green Man, is still serving drinks but Mason's Orphanage and the Jaffray Hospital buildings became superfluous to modern needs and have been demolished. Nearly all of the farmhouses and cottages photographed here have gone, as have the High Street cinemas, though the new multiplex cinema on the Kingsbury Road offers more choice than was ever available in the first heyday of cinema going.

From a conservation stance it could have been a lot worse. While the large Victorian houses which fronted the Sutton Road between the High Street and Wylde Green were swept away to build the Lyndhurst Estate, even more ambitious developments were thwarted. There were plans to build a multi-storey development on the Green in the 1960s and permission was also sought to demolish the Abbey and also to build on Pype Hayes Park on land vacated by the prefabs along the Chester Road.

Although Erdington has had its fair share of housing estates they are scattered around the district so that the predominant feature of the suburb is one of mixed character. Victorian, Edwardian and later houses and roads co-exist and most of the street scenes recorded here are instantly recognizable today even if the street furniture and transport belong to a distant age. The Village Green, the Six Ways and the High Street, despite the half-hearted pedestrianisation, are still the focal ponts of community life and shopping. The area's physical characteristics have, though, largely vanished under the pressure of bricks and tarmac. Who would now recognize Gravelly Hill from its physical description as 'a region of thick forest rising steeply from the River Tame' or locate the site of the cave dwellings or 'dwarf holes'.

Part of the pleasure of choosing photographs for this book has been the challenge of identifying the scenes but, as well, there has been the delight of recreating aspects of the recent history of Erdington. Writing at the beginning of the photographic age a correspondent to the Erdington Monthly Recorder looked forward to a day when Erdington would have justice done to it. 'It will wake up to find itself in one of those popular magazines, in all the glory of "small pica" and a dozen "process blocks". Thence forward, thro' all ages, it will remain famous.' The authors hope that this collection goes some way at least towards achieving these grandiose aims. The one regret is that too little of Erdington's industrial and working life is reflected in this anthology. Very few photographs of factories and working scenes have found their way to the photographic collections in Birmingham Central Library. Perhaps some will emerge, if so they will be warmly welcomed as indeed would any other photographs of Erdington.

To balance the relative scarcity of industrial photographs the compilers have had one inestimable advantage in their task. This is that one of the great pioneers of the early days of photography, Sir John Benjamin Stone, made his home in Erdington and captured for posterity, life there at the turn of the century. It is fitting that this introduction as well as the selection of photographs ends with a tribute to this great photograper whose entire collection is now freely available for all to see in Birmingham Central Library.

One
Rural Erdington

Holifast Farm, 1893.

Holifast Farm house, Chester Road. When offered for auction in 1898 the estate was described as 'Holifast Grange, a Queen Anne residence, with carriage drive, well belted with old fir and beech trees, having also gardens, orchard and farmery, and meadow together with Holifast Grange Farm adjoining , the whole occupying upwards of 68 acres.' The estate had last been offered for sale in 1877.

Rear view of Holifast Farm house, 1893.

Holifast Farm yard, 1892.

Entrance to Pype Hayes Park, 1894.

Braggington Fields, 1931. The fields were known after Simeon Braggington, a dairyman who farmed Moor End Lane farm in the 1920s and '30s. The farm was turned into Dunvegan Road estate around 1934, although the farmhouse survived until 1968.

Rick fire at the corner of Chester Road and Grange Lane, July 1893.

Terry's Lane, 1893.

Terry's Lane.

Little Pitts Farm, Chester Road. All traces of the farm were obliterated when a new estate off the Chester Road was built in 1961. The stabling was eighteenth century, but the house had been rebuilt later. The Pitts were holes between the Farm and the nearby Chester Road, probably made by digging for sand and gravel for nearby Pype Hayes Hall. One such hole still exists inside the park. Perhaps the preservation of the double 'tt' showed that the authorities imagined it derived from a personal name.

Erdington Hall farm buildings, 1892.

Dwarf Holes, Gravelly Hill. The caves were the only place in Birmingham with a strong claim to Stone Age connections. They consisted of two or more holes carved out of sandstone and gave access to large artificial caves. Rediscovered about 1900 they were too waterlogged to explore. Later when sewage work was being carried out nearby they were blocked up. What exploration was possible showed that they were partly the work of man. A deed of 1490 refers to several parcels of land including two crofts of land called Dwarffenholes. Locals used the caves as air raid shelters in World War Two. They were destroyed when Spaghetti Junction was built in 1973.

Moat Cottages on the site where Moat Farm bordered onto Moor End Lane. This black and white half-timbered building was an early barn conversion from Moat Farm's outbuildings. The farm and the Moat House were demolished in 1935 to make way for the Berkswell Road estate, but the cottages still had a sitting tenant. To accommodate the tenant the building was guillotined off just to the right of the black infill in the centre and this curious structure remained a feature of Moor End Lane until 1962 when it was demolished to make way for an MEB sub-station.

Shipley Cottages which stood in Moor End Lane just to the east of what is now Berkswell Road. They were named after Shipley Fields.

Number 2 Fern Road stood at the corner of Church Road. A late eighteenth-century cottage, it was built on what was originally waste land, before the enclosures took place. Until 1944-1945 this was a thatched cottage and it was said to be the last so roofed in Birmingham. The thatch was replaced because of the risk of fire from bomb damage.

Keepers Cottage, Pype Hayes, 1894.

Gardeners Cottages, Chester Road, 1894.

Cottages, Terry's Lane, 1893.

Rustic Cottage, Sutton Road. Number 63 dated back to around 1500 with additions to the original house being added in the seventeenth century. Records show that it stood in 1547. Situated by Holly Lane, the quaint black and white structure was a local feature and the oldest house in Erdington before it was demolished on 26 November 1955 to make way for a new house built further from the roadside.

Rose Cottage, Holly Lane, a farmhouse of the mid-eighteenth century. At that period it stood on a grassy island as Grange Lane bifurcated to meet Holly Lane. Rose Cottage was used as a nursery from 1833 for over a hundred years. The cottage was latterly known as Ricketts Farm with pigs and turkeys kept there until its demolition to make way for the building of Avalon Close.

Early eighteenth-century cottages at Wood End Lane, 14 August 1955.

Station Road Cottages. Many of the old houses and cottages in Station Road, formerly Sheep Street, were demolished. Numbers 23-25 have been restored. Station Road was an ancient way from Rowden Green (the village green was originally known as Roden's End) via Marsh Lane to Stockland Green and Witton.

Berwood Cottages, Chester Road. Berwood Cottages were of seventeenth-century origins. There were ten cottages in all, standing sideways to the road on the site of Yenton Court near Sutton Road. Number 740 was the last and was demolished in 1957 when the Chester Road was widened.

Old Cottages, High Street. This old house stood at the back of Easy Row. Easy Row stood opposite the National School on the High Street. Probably the oldest cottage or house in the village, it stood approximately on the site of the present day Woolworths. The cottage is quite dilapidated in this Benjamin Stone photograph.

Two
Grand Houses

Erdington Hall.

Erdington Hall Farm from the canal bank looking north-east.

Erdington Hall farmyard, 1911.

Erdington Hall was demolished around 1912 when land was needed for the building of the Tyburn Road. The Hall stood near to Abbotts Road between Wheelwright Road and Tyburn Road. The original manor house would have been a large fortified building, moated on three sides and on the fourth defended by the River Tame. The building known as Erdington Hall was probably built in the sixteen hundreds and was the residence of the Jennings family. Another of its well-known owners was Sir Lister Holte. In 1858 the Hall was occupied by William Wheelwright, a farmer, who may well have given his name to Wheelwright Road.

The ancient Pipe Manor House was the home of William Maunsell in the eleventh century. The original house stood near Wood Lane. It was later rebuilt around 1600 and became the home of the Holden family. It was a half-timbered gabled house, possibly being the oldest house in Erdington for a while.

The back of Pipe Hall, 1899. The
house was demolished in 1932.

Pipe Hall. A Jacobean open
fireplace, 1899.

Old moat at Pipe Hall, 1899.

The Dovecote at Pipe Hall, 1931.

The modern lodge to Pype Hayes Hall, Chester Road. It would appear that the two old cottages opposite the Bagot Arms were originally the entrance. The road entering the park on this view was a public highway two centuries ago and emerged over the bridge in Eachelhurst Road.

The house of the thirteen gables, Pype Hayes Hall dates back to the sixteen hundreds and the Bagot family. In the early seventeenth century Harvey Bagot married Dorothy Arden, daughter of Sir Henry Arden, and was given the Pipe Lands as a dowry. His father built the house for him in the days of James I, imparking a portion of the waste common land, and encircling it by a fence; hence the name Pype Hayes. Hayes means an enclosure and the house was built in the Manor of Pype.

Pype Hayes Hall, 1884. The original house was much altered in the eighteenth century. In 1906 the Hall was sold to a local industrialist James Rollason, a wire manufacturer. In 1919 the house was purchased by Birmingham City Council for £10,000. It became a nursery for children in care. Today it is used by the Social Services Department of Birmingham City Council.

Woodcutter, Pype Hayes Hall. Twenty-one trees were blown down during the storm of February 1894.

The lodge to Rookery House, 1904.

The Rookery, September 1904. Rookery House was built between 1725 and 1730, by Abraham Spooner, and was known as Birches Green. Until 1905 it was a family home surrounded by private gardens. Over the years a succession of owners changed, extended and repaired the house. Under the ownership of the Wiley family the name of the house was changed to The Rookery in September 1904.

The gardens of Rookery House. In 1905 Rookery House was sold by Doctor Paget Evans, a local councillor to the Erdington Urban Dsitrict Council. It became 'The Council House' and the gardens were opened to the public as Rookery Park, Erdington's first public park, in 1905.

Three
Public Buildings

Library and Village Green, 1969.

At a meeting of the Erdington Urban District Council in 1907 Mr Charles Smith said he 'thought the time had arrived when Erdington should possess a library of its own.' His colleagues, however, thought differently. Mr Smith wrote to millionaire Andrew Carnegie, who generously offered a gift of £5,000. After a further gift from Mr Carnegie the library was built and opened on 2 July 1907. The original plans for a Civic Centre, including the swimming baths in the same building were not carried out because of lack of funds. A penny rate was levied to meet the cost of the upkeep. The first librarian, Mr E.W. Neesham, was appointed in January 1908.

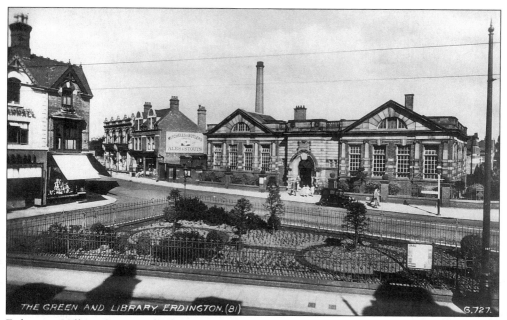

Erdington Village Green and Library, c. 1932.

Erdington Library. Interior showing bookshelves.

The entrance hall of Erdington Library, 1913.

The counters at Erdington, January, 1959.

Sutton New Road and the Post Office, built in 1934, seen here in 1950.

Sutton New Road and the Post Office.

In 1818 a Parliamentary grant led to the building of a church in Erdington. The cost of the church was around £6,500, of which £1,000 was raised by subscriptions of the inhabitants. *Aris' Birmingham Gazette* on Monday 17 June quotes 'On Tuesday morning the first stone of a new chapel from the designs and under the supervision of Messrs Richman and Hutchinson of this town was laid in due form by the Right Honourable Earl Howe...' Gothic in design, the church took two years to build. The church of St Barnabas was consecrated on 23 July 1824. Until this date Erdington people had to travel to Aston to worship. In 1858 Erdington became a separate ecclesiastical parish of its own.

The interior of St Barnabas, 1900. The church was greatly enlarged in 1883, with seating for 1,100 persons. The first ministers were curates of Aston. The first vicar, Revd Hyla Holden Rose, lived in Edgbaston for several years, travelling to Erdington to conduct the services until the new vicarage was built in 1860.

View from the church tower, 1900.

The Abbey from the front. "St. Thomas". Erdington.

In 1847 Father Heneage built a chapel in the High Street, on the croft opposite the end of Station Lane. Before this priests from Oscott had said mass in a house on the High Street, but Catholics in Erdington are mainly indebted to the Revd Daniel H. Haigh, founder of the Church of St Thomas & St Edmund. He laid the foundation stone of the new church on 26 May 1848. The church was opened and consecrated by Bishop Ullathorne on 11 June. The church is usually considered one of the best examples of the Gothic revivial.

Built by Charles Hansom, the steeple of the church is 117 ft high, which is also the length of the building. In 1876 Father Haigh handed over his church, parish and estate of four acres to the Benedictine monks from Beuron in Germany, exiled for their faith from their own country.

At the rear of St Thomas about 1910, looking towards Rowden Hill and Sutton Road. This drive survived until the Lyndhurst estate was built.

Pilgrimage to Erdington Abbey, 5 August 1906.

Originally the old Congregational Chapel in Bell Lane (now Orphanage Road), the building was used as a police station before becoming the Parochial Rooms. Today it is the site of the fire station. It was the home of a founder member of the Erdington Athletic Club, Mr George F. Garrison. When he lived there he remembered one cell was converted into a soup kitchen where his mother made soup in a 40 gallon gas furnace and distributed it among the poor.

The Baptist church, 1889. In 1877 a group of Baptists held meetings in the old public hall. The following year a church was formally enrolled. Later that year a site was secured at the corner of High Street and Birches Green Road, now Wood End Road. The cost, including church building and land, was £1,800. Extensions were added in 1884, 1889, 1893 and 1907. The church closed in 1958 and was demolished in 1961.

The Methodist church. In 1858, when Josiah Mason built his first orphanage in Station Road he permitted the Methodists to use the large hall there. Services were held until 1868 when a scheme was launched for building a chapel near the new railway line. In 1902 the second chapel opened. It was altered in 1922 and extended in 1931.

In 1811 the Wesleyans decided to provide a place of worship in Erdington. A cottage in Bell Lane was registered for this purpose, the first minister being the Revd Mark H. Mogridge. The cottage was sold to the Congregationalists for £315 in 1822. In 1813 a chapel was built on land adjoining the cottage. In 1837 work began on the new Congregational church in the High Street. The church was 56 ft long by 32 ft wide, with seating for 350. A schoolroom was made under the chapel. The building cost £1,500 and the first service was held on 3 July 1838. This photograph shows the church and the back of Mason's Almshouses in Station Road before it became the Greek Orthodox church.

The old Wesleyan Church, Station Road, 1901, before the new one was built in front of it.

The Mission Hall, April, 1937.

John Jaffray was born in Stirling, Scotland in 1818 and was educated at Glasgow High School. He came to England as a reporter and to Birmingham in 1844 to take up a post on the *Birmingham Journal*. Jaffray proved to have a good business brain as well as a literary power and John Fenney, a proprietor of the newspaper decided to make him a partner in 1852. Within a few years Jaffray began to make his mark in town as a business and public figure. He was connected with nearly all the movements in Birmingham, whether it was politics, the arts, literature or philanthropy. By the time of his death in 1901 he had accumulated a great deal of wealth, and had become a baronet.

The Jaffray Hospital, standing in eight acres of grounds was built and equipped by John Jaffray, and was opened by the Prince of Wales (later Edward VIII) on 29 November 1885, as a place where the helpless would be properly looked after and brought back to good health.

Laying the foundation stone of Jaffray Hospital, 1884.

An artist's view of Jaffray Hospital, 1884.

Four
The Orphanage

Josiah Mason Orphanage from Grange Lane, 1895.

View from gardens, 1896. Josiah Masons Orphanage had two towers, one with a clock which struck the hours and annoyed nearby residents. The orphanage was visible for miles around, sited as it was on the old Erdington ridge. It fronted on to Bell Lane (Orphanage Road) and opened in 1869. It survived as an orphanage and later a school, open to day-pupils, until it was demolished in 1963. The Yenton Primary Schools and the estate centred on Goodison Gardens now occupy this site.

View of the orphanage with the mortuary chapel, 1908.

Mortuary Chapel, 1908. Services in the main chapel were usually conducted by Wesleyan Methodist Ministers. Local people were also welcomed in the chapel and they used the gallery which seated 200.

Mason Orphanage Burial Place. 1908. The mausoleum was pulled down in January 1964 to provide room for extensions to the Yenton Primary School. Two years earlier the bodies of Mason, his wife and 54 orphanage children had been removed from the grounds and cremated at Perry Barr crematorium.

The orphanage viewed from the road.

The view from the tower looking to Grange Lane, 1899.

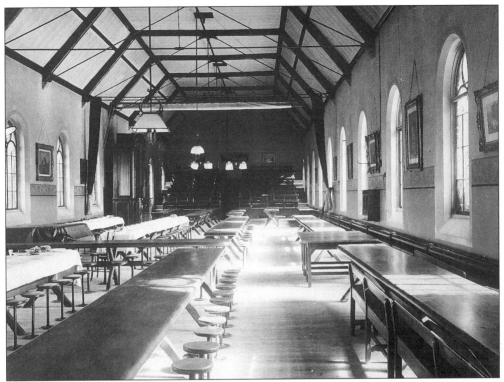

The dining room, 1908. The massive dining hall linked the main building with the dormitories. It was capable of seating 500 children although the maximum housed at the orphanage was 350 in 1889.

The dining room, 1937.

The gymnasium, September 1908.

Recreation, 1937.

The playing fields, 1937.

The swimming pool, 1937. After Mason's death the trustees attempted to make the orphanage more homely and less of an institution. There was more time for sport and the swimming pool was built in 1889.

Children at play, 1937.

A nurse with a boy in the dayroom of the sick quarters, 1937.

Boys in school at the orphanage, with the master Mr Reid, 1908.

Group of the Trustees of Mason's Orphanage, 1908. According to Sir Josiah Mason's wishes the trustees had to be laymen, Protestants and living within ten miles of the orphanage. After Mason's death, Birmingham Town Council appointed seven of the trustees. The trustees acted as a Board of Management for the orphanage and its estate.

The founder of the orphanage was born in Kidderminster in 1795 and died at his Erdington home, close to the orphanage in 1881. He was the epitome of the Victorian entrepreneur and philanthropist using the wealth from his successful pen making business to fund the orphanage and Mason Science College, the forerunner of Birmingham University.

Josiah Mason's wife, Anne, was his cousin and was said to share his virtues of frugality and hard work. Their marriage was childless but lasted for 52 years until her death in 1870.

A statue of Mason stood in Chamberlain Place in the city centre for 65 years. It suffered damage over the years including losing its right hand. The bust part was recreated in bronze and erected on the Chester Road-Orphanage Road crossing, facing the site of the orphanage.

Five

High Street and
The Village Green

Village green and High Street.

Six Ways Erdington, c. 1910.

Six Ways Erdington, c. 1919. Note the original Queens Head. Archer's stores is on the right.

Six Ways looking towards Gravelly Hill.

Six Ways, about 1925 when the roundabout had just been made. The trams loaded on the island. Archer's stores were taken down shortly after this photograph.

The roundabout at Six Ways before it was made into a raised garden, May 1956. It claimed to be the first traffic roundabout in the country. Paynes shop marks the site of Archer's grocery stores. Jones' garage had just been taken over by the Abbey garage.

Six Ways Erdington looking towards Sutton New Road and the High Street, September, 1938.

High Street, April 1928.

High Street prior to the removal of the trams to Sutton New Road, May 1938.

High Street from Station Road. The old Post Office is by the first lamp post on the right.

The High Street before the removal of the top storey of the Acorn Hotel, c. 1938. The tram lines have been roughly covered.

Burton's, the tailors, High Street, photographed in the 1950s.

High Street and the corner of New Road, May 1953.

Church House, c. 1919. The Church House foundation stone was laid 14 June 1911. The Britannic was probably in the building from the beginning but the shop on the left has changed hands many times.

Looking along the High Street towards the Village Green on a busy Saturday afternoon, c. 1948.

Taken about 1954 looking towards Newman Road Church. Jones' garage had been bought by
Abbey garage. Note the very old house between the garage and the key shop. This was the
house of the foreman in charge of the now vanished smithy.

An early view of the High Street.

Erdington High Street looking towards the Village Green.

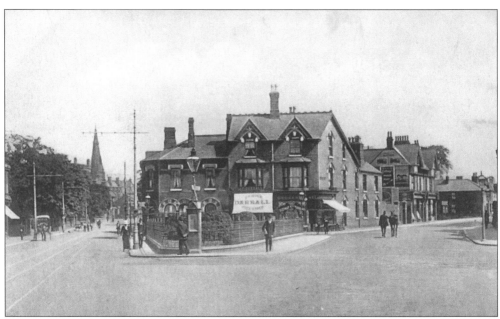

Erdington Village Green about 1918. On the right of Darrall's is Lett's grocery and on the left is Dean's drapery. The trees on the left are standing in 'The Grove' next to the Congregational Church.

The Village Green.

Sunday scene at the Erdington Village Green, 2 December 1956. The horse-drawn milk cart is owned by the Co-op and Shufflebotham's store on the left was converted into the 'outdoor' for the Swan Inn.

The Village Green timber and garden stores.

The Village Green and Public Library, c. 1948.

Six
Roads and Houses

Early view of the High Street and Station Road with the Abbey in the background.

Number 29 Station Road, December 1955. A mid eighteenth century house, whose outhouses had timber framing, and served an even older farmhouse, along side what used to be called Sheep Street, before the railway was built.

Edwards Road, 1960s. High Street and Station Street junction.

Abbey Cottages, numbers 1 to 23, Sutton Road, 1955. The houses differ in design, but are all of the eighteenth century, some dating back to c. 1740. The steps had handrails until the last war. The house on the extreme right with the bay window used to be a grocery shop.

Sutton Road. Cottages, butchers shop and garage, opposite the Abbey.

An early view of Sutton Road.

Willmot House, Sutton Road, December 1955. Once a sixteenth century farmhouse of the Benbow family. George Willmot lived here at the beginning of the last century.

The building of the Sutton New Road and the corner of Coton Lane, March 1938. Coton Road was divided into two roads by the building of the new road.

Sutton New Road looking north from North Road, during alterations, March 1938. The Post Office was built in 1934.

Sutton New Road, June 1938. The chemist shop was the last to be demolished.

The old Post Office and shop in the High Street before demolition, July 1937.

Old houses, Sutton Road, just beyond the Village Green.

Number 66 Sutton Road. One of the Lyndhurst estate houses before demolition. The demolition of the old houses and the building of the estate was a unique experiment in 1959-60.

Number 78 Sutton Road. Houses of substance and character such as Parkfield House, residence of a past Lord Mayor Thomas O. Williams, Normanhurst, once Mrs Guest's Maternity Home, Wilmot House, Stanley House and Beechmont, once a private hotel were demolished as their leases ran out.

Number 76 Sutton Road just prior to demolition, November 1956. In all nearly twenty properties were destroyed. The land which was owned by the Walter Stanley Trust totalled some thirty eight acres. Plans were drawn up for housing, open space, road improvements, primary school and an aged persons' home.

The Lyndhurst estate, c. 1960. The estate was launched in May 1960 with great ceremony. The Primary School was opened by Lord Morrison of Lambeth, and the first Headmaster was Mr C. Walker.

Aerial view of Lyndhurst estate, 1961. Harlech Tower was the first sixteen-story block of flats to be erected in Birmingham. The estate won a Civic Trust Amenity Award.

Looking towards Sutton near Holly Lane, 1919. On the left is the entrance to one of the early Victorian houses and on the right is Rustic Cottage (Jos Avery, builder). This was once the house of Richard Wright who died here in 1542, 'one nook of land' with the house. The house was demolished by Mr Bond in November 1955.

Sutton Road before alterations, May 1938.

Sutton Road and Chester Road. This tram, number 695, was built in 1925.

Sutton Road and Chester Road junction during alterations, May 1938.

Chester Road and Sutton Road junction before the tram lines were removed. Chester Road is one of the oldest roads in Erdington and probably predated the Romans. It is literally the road to Chester which is seventy three miles from Pype Hayes.

Two views of Chester Road near Pype Hayes Park entrance, May 1932.

Chester Road 'prefabs', 1951. Officially called 'temporary bungalows' they were built for as little as £800 as an answer to the post-war housing crisis. Designed to last ten years they became much loved and were not pulled down until the early 1980s. Despite proposals to build on the site, the land reverted back to Pype Hayes Park.

Chester Road near Pype Hayes before the road was widened.

Numbers 1063 to 1065 Chester Road, 1957. On a map of 1760 these cottages are marked as lodges to Pypes Hayes Hall. After falling vacant these two cottages were eventually made into one.

Eversley, Farthing Lane, off Kingsbury Road, c. 1905. For many years the home of the Whittall's, the house stood opposite the Old Green Man. It is shown on a map dated 1760 as a farmhouse. After being empty for many years it was demolished in 1952.

Kingsbury Road, September 1904. The driver of the horse and trap is Fred Bass who later became caretaker at Rookery House and lived in a flat there with his family. The erection of this sign on the site of the old Glenthorne estate led to a major outcry from local residents. The proposal to build the gas works was defeated and the Birches Green estate now occupies the site.

Glenthorne, 1896.

Glenthorne, 1985.

Kingsbury Road and Tyburn Road junction, 1933.

Kingsbury Road and Tyburn Road. The Norton Public house is on the right. 1935.

Tyburn Road, 1922.

Tyburn Road, 1928.

Eachelhurst Road near the city boundary and Sutton Coldfield, March 1934.

Eachelhurst Road near the city boundary. Pype Hayes Park is on the right, 1934.

Terry's Lane, 1893. Terry's Lane is now Eachelhurst Lane. The snow scene shows Mr Thomas Terry and is taken looking towards Walmley. The trees on the left are part of Pype Hayes Park.

Grange Road looking towards The Cedars, the residence of Mr W. Greener, February 1895.

Mr Greener's pool at The Cedars. Mr Greener, a gunmaker, later lived at Blaknalls, the black and white timbered house on Grange Road from 1904 to 1920. He owned a considerable amount of land in Erdington. Poppy Lane was originally called Greeners' Lane.

Miss Greener at The Cedars, Grange Road, 1899.

The Cedars, 1899.

The Dovecote at The Cedars, 1985.

Grange Road near the entrance to The Grange (now the John Taylor Hospice), 1896. Called Pipe Hayes Lane in 1651 the road adopted its current name after The Grange house. It was a narrow tree shaded lane until the turn of the century with only three houses, The Grange, Blaknalls (both still surviving) and a derelict cottage long gone. It was called Grange Lane until Erdington was taken over by Birmingham Council in 1911.

Holly Lane near the junction with Orphanage Road, 1892.

Holly Lane and Nocks Brickworks, 1931. The brickworks were a prominent landmark in Erdington for nearly one hundred years from 1878. The site closed in 1965 after the last of the clay had been extracted. Many Erdington houses and the Dunlop works were built with bricks from the Holly Lane factory. The two 150 ft high chimneys were a feature of Erdington life from 1920.

Cotton's Farmhouse which stood on the corner of Orphanage Road and Blythe Lane (the top of Holly Lane), 1893.

Orphanage Road, 1894. In the centre is the house of Mr and Mrs Hopkins. Previously called Hogge Street and then Bell Lane the road became known as Orphanage Road in 1903 after Mason's Orphanage was built.

Numbers 66-70 Orphanage Road, 1955. The trade sign is for Mr Hunt the sweep. In 1760 the row of cottages was in the tenure of Newby and Brown and in 1833 there were five houses, the near end of the three remaining ones shows where the other two stood.

The junction of Edwards Road and Orphanage Road. A modern day car park now stands on the site of the old cottages.

Station Road, June 1926.

Church Road, Erdington.

Church Road, 1920. On the left, behind the fence is the vicarage. On the right is the entrance to 'The Cottages', an old farmhouse. The lower part of Church Road only existed as a narrow cart track until this century. The original name of the track and road has been lost but it probably took the name of the farm.

The Cottage, Church Road was once a substantial farmhouse dating back to the 1720s. It was used as a citizens club during the 1939-45 war. This rear view shows the kitchens. Church Road is older than the church but it was not named until 1900. It only went as far as Moor End to the Green Man Inn on the High Street (later The Acorn).

The Cottage, Church Road, 1894.

Coton Lane, 1935.

York Road, 1935.

Erdington Laundry, Summer Road. Erdington Laundry was officially opened in December 1898 and became a major enterprise in Erdington employing over 200 people. The building as well as thousands of bundles of family washing were destroyed in a fire on 2 March 1954.

Summer Road and the corner of Six Ways, 1935.

Gravelly Lane looking towards Chester Road. Gravelly Lane appears on a 1760 map of Erdington flanked on both sides by fields. The enclosures in the early nineteenth century altered the site of the junction with Goosemoor Lane.

Court Lane looking towards Oscott College, c. 1948. On the left is Jerrys' Lane.

Norfolk Road looking towards Court Lane, c. 1948.

Somerset Road looking towards Court Lane, c. 1948. The houses on the right have very ornamental name plaques interspersed with heraldic signs.

Goosemoor Lane, c. 1948. Stones' Garden Laundry was taken over by the Co-operative Society. The entrance on the left led to a pathway leading across allotments into Court Lane. Until the 1801 enclosure the road ran to the Chester Road rather than Court Lane. It derived its name from the surrounding lands called Goosemoor, probably after fields of gorse.

Marsh Hill. The outer circle bus route ran up Marsh Hill. On the left is the Special School. The allotments behind the shop were on land belonging to Grove Farm, which stood opposite Witton Hall, taken down in 1962.

Laburnum Cottages, Turfpits Lane, 1955.

Short Heath Road. Short Heath was built in 1820 by George Wells. The centre window was the original 'Chapel' where the first mass since the Reformation in this Parish was held. Alterations have now completely changed this house.

Gypsy Lane, 1925. An old road but not named until the end of the nineteenth century, it derives its name from the gypsies who used it to reach the Chester Road after visiting the Aston onion fairs.

Gypsy Lane, 1925.

Perry Common Road, 1925.

Harman Road looking towards Sutton Road, c. 1928. Named after John Harman a benefactor of Sutton Coldfield who became Bishop Vesey.

Harman Road extension, 1938.

Burlington House, Copeley Hill, 1894.

Parkfield House, Gravelly Hill, 1899.

Dr. Crabbe and his family. Copeley Hill, 1895.

A view from Copeley Hill in the winter of 1895, looking across the River Tame near Salford Bridge.

Seven

Transport

Tram on Gravelly Hill, 1953.

The building of the tramway on Gravelly Hill. By the Tramway Act of 1902 the Erdington Council was permitted to construct tramways within their district. The tramway number 1 from Salford Bridge to Wylde Green which ran up Gravelly Hill was opened in April 1907.

Looking from Reservoir Road to the High Street, 1938.

Laying the new tramway crossover on the Sutton New Road, 1938.

Sutton New Road from Wilton Road, 1938.

High Street and Sutton New Road, 1938.

Erdington tram terminus at Wylde Green. Sutton Coldfield Council voted not to have trams running through Sutton Coldfield so the Birmingham trams only reached the Sutton boundary, just beyond the junction of Chester Road and Sutton Road.

The trams ran for forty six years. The last tram to Chester Road and, the last one in Birmingham, outside Josiah Masons almshouse on the way to the terminus. It left Chester Road for Miller Street depot on Saturday 4 July 1953, ending a remarkable era of transport. All overhead wires were taken down during the night of 9 July and the new mobile buses took over.

Erdington's first bus on the 64 route, following in the wake of the last tram, July 1953. Erdington's the chemist is on the right and also the site of Grove House shops and offices.

STOCKLAND GREEN BUS TERMINUS.

Stockland Green Bus Terminus. The Erdington to Acocks Green section of what became the outer circle route opened on 15 January 1923, using one-man, twenty seater buses. The outer circle was completed in 1926 and single deck buses were soon replaced by double-deckers because of the popularity of the route. The Tyburn Road service garage was opened in December 1929. This photograph was taken from outside the newly opened Fondella Confectioners shop. Wilkinson's chemists is behind the bus and Slade Road is beyond.

Chester Road Railway Station, 1933. Castle Bromwich Station was situated on the Midland Railway line which ran through Sutton Coldfield to Aldridge and Wolverhampton. The route between Castle Bromwich and Wolverhampton was built as two sections. The first, Wolverhampton to Walsall opened in 1872 and the Walsall to Castle Bromwich section opened on the 1 July 1879.

Chester Road Railway Station. The passenger service on the Walsall to Castle Bromwich section ceased on 18 January 1865, but the line is still used today for freight.

The Birmingham and Fazeley Canal from Tyburn Bridge, 1892. The Erdington Canal is in reality about a four mile stretch of the Birmingham and Fazeley Canal. The canal was completed in 1790. A walk or cycle ride from Hansons Bridge to Salford Bridge still gives a fascinating view of Erdington's industrial history.

The canal tollhouse on Chester Road, 1955.

Eight

Leisure

Fishing, Pype Hayes park, c. 1940.

Erdington Picture House, 1956. The cinema closed on 1 December 1956. It was often referred to as West's Picture House. The chemists shop on the left was previously Wilton's hence Wilton Road nearby. On the right are the grounds of the Swan Inn.

The Palace Cinema, 1952. The Palace showing its first film on Boxing Day 1912. It was previously the People's Hall and was used for a variety of leisure activities. The sprung maple dance floor was one of the best in the country and the ballroom was used for regular weekly radio broadcasts. The musical *Oliver* was the cinema's last showing before it closed down in August 1972.

The Old Green Man, 1899. Often known by its slang name 'The Lad in the lane' this public house claims to be the oldest in Warwickshire. Some of its beams have marks believed to date from 1306, although most of the building dates from the sixteenth century. The Old Green Man was renamed The Lad in the Lane in 1971 when it was renovated, but due to popular demand it soon reverted back to The Old Green Man.

The rear of the Old Green Man, 1899.

The Old Green Man in 1939.

The Cross Keys. The present inn was built in 1911 on the site of two old cottages which stood in front of the old inn. The old inn was an eighteenth century house subsequently converted to an inn. The Cross Keys stands at the corner of the High Street and Station Road.

The Queens Head, Six Ways Erdington, c. 1900. Originally a fairly small coaching inn of early Victorian date, it was pulled down in the 1930s and new inn was built further back from the road.

The Old White Lion, 102 High Street, 1956.

The Roebuck. The Roebuck dates back to 1760 and was originally called the Bull's Head. In 1791 the landlord was shot and killed by travellers. The legend 'Halfway House' was written on the wall as it was mid-way between Birmingham and the Four Oaks racecourse. The inn was pulled down in 1965 as part of the High Street improvements and the new inn was opened in 1967.

The Stocklands, c. 1928. A very early picture of the hotel, before the heavy chains were places between the pillars. Built in 1924, the building preceded most of the new houses around. Stockland farm, an eighteenth-century building stood close to this site.

The Swan Inn public house, 1952.

The Swan on the High Street dates from the early eighteenth century and is little altered on this frontage. Notice the old lamps. At the rear are very old stables once used by the old time coach house. The Littlehales family owned the inn for many generations.

The Swan Inn in the course of demolition. The older wing remains on the left, also the original Post Office along side which used to be Littlehayes Stores.

The Tyburn House, 1910. An early eighteenth-century hostelry which features in the Mary Ashford murder case of 1817 as the venue for the dance. It was pulled down in 1930.

The new Tyburn House was built with a large dance hall catering for 220 and is now used as a restaurant.

Pype Hayes Hall, the park and various outbuildings were purchased by Birmingham Parks Committee from the Bagot Trustees in 1919 for £10,000. The land was acquired for playing fields to compensate for the loss of the Castle Bromwich playing fields which had been acquired by the War Office for an aerodrome. The park was officially opened on 24 March 1920.

The pools in Pype Hayes Park, 1894.

Completed pool improvement works, 1959.

Pype Hayes Park and shelter.

PIPE HAYES PARK, ERDINGTON.   H.1161.

Pype Hayes Park and shelter. A 1935 view looking from the pool to the Hall, with the rose garden on the right, behind the keeper's shelter.

The pool at Pype Hayes Park, 1894.

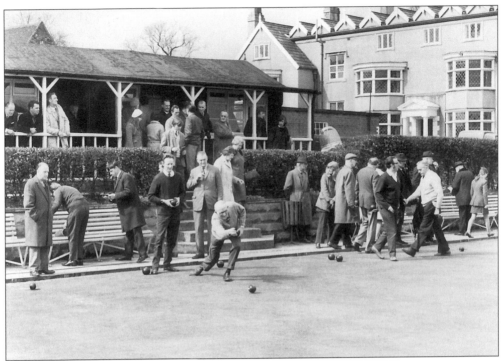

Playing Bowls in the park, 1970.

Pype Hayes Hall and gardens, 1966.

Rookery House and gardens. Rookery House was sold to the Erdington Urban District Council in 1905. The house became the Council House for Erdington and the gardens were opened to the public as Rookery Park, Erdington's first public park in 1905.

Rookery Park, 1924.

Brookvale Park, 1951. The brick jetty with rails visible between the two lakes. These are the remnants of the seventeenth century Spade Mill. In 1909 Erdington District Council bought the old reservoir below George Road which had fallen out of use when the Welsh Water Scheme was completed and created a new public path.

The bandstand at Brookvale Park, c. 1918. The fields in the distance became Witton Allotments in 1920. The house at the rear of the bandstand dates to about 1870, and between it and the bandstand is a brick pier jutting out into the water. These are the remnants of the old mill which stood here for some three centuries.

The rustic bridge over the paddling pool, 1951. At one time the park boasted an open air swimming pool as well as the boathouse and bandstand.

The bandstands and bowling green, c. 1928. In the distance are the huts on Witton allotments and on the right is the spire of the chapel in Witton Cemetery.

Witton Lakes, Erdington.

Witton Lakes were acquired by Birmingham Corporation in 1914 as a fishing reserve. They were opened as a park in 1926. In the distance is the causeway which divides the large and small pools. Across this a road runs from the top of Bleak Hill Road to somewhere near Perry Bridge. This photograph was taken c. 1951

Witton Lakes, August 1955. A water mill stood at the lower end of the larger lake on the left. The fields in the distance on the right hand side are now covered by the Wyrley Birch estate flats.

Nine
Sir Benjamin Stone Miscellany

Sir Benjamin Stone the photographer.

Grange Lane and the drive to The Grange, 1908. Benjamin Stone bought The Grange in 1877. He extended the property and purchased adjoining land until it comprised five and a half acres. The Grange was the Stones' family home until his death and was a fitting country seat for a manufacturer and local politician.

The Grange, 1877. The estate agent's description of 1919 gives a picture of the house. 'The land in front contains a large number of forest trees and has a sloping lawn from the windows of the dinning and drawing rooms... porched and titled entrance hall, morning room, drawing room, dining room, billiard room, smoking room, housemaid's pantry, glass pantry, housekeeper's room, kitchen, two cellars, scullery, bathroom, five large bedrooms, two maids rooms, box room and observatory, nursery, library, underground fernery, outside fernery and adjoining hall, motor house (heated with hot pipes) accomodating two motors, workshop, stables for two horses (including loft, harness room, loose box and two stall stable) coach house for two carriages, conservatory, potting shed, flower garden, full size tennis lawn, kitchen garden, orchard and external shrubbery etc.'

The Grange.

The drive to The Grange in snow, 1892.

The drawing room, 1897. The records, letters and notebooks from Sir Benjamin's travels abroad tell us as much about him as a person as about his photographic subject matter. In a note book in which he planned his holiday in Medoc, France, he listed his requirements for his journey. They numbered 83 items including: 18 handkerchiefs, hammer, teeth box, eye glass, 2 candles, umbrella, night shirt and medal! A separate list of photographic matter includes 27 dark slides, 210 plates in all, extra metal legs and sample photograph. He lists several camera bags and how each one should be packed for the journey.

The drawing room, 1897.

The library, 1896.

The garden at The Grange, 1894.
The Orphanage tower can just be
seen through the trees on the right.

The gardens in winter, 1900.

Mr F. H. Pepper and his children make a morning call at The Grange, 1903.

East Birmingham election workers at a political garden party at The Grange, 29 July 1901.

Thomas Barnsley J.P. a trustee of
Mason's Orphanage, 1908.

Mr and Mrs Oscar H. Stone, and two train bearers, after their wedding. Oscar was the fifth child
of the Stone family. They had six children, four boys and two girls.

Lady Jane Stone on Christmas Day, 1909. Very little is known about Jane. He married her on 5 June 1867 at the age of 29 and, Jane Parker was ten years his junior. She seems to have left all the limelight to John Benjamin, content to remain at home during her husband's often prolonged trips abroad. According to one press cutting in the Stone collection, Jane was an extremely popular woman among her friends both in London and in Birmingham.

John Benjamin Stone was born on 9 February 1838. He died in 1914 at the end of the Victorian Edwardian era which he had recorded for posterity through his photographs. During his life time he was a politician, collector, traveller, social worker, geologist, astronomer, botanist, glass and paper manufacturer, author and lecturer. He was knighted in 1892 and from 1895 to 1909 he was Member of Parliament for East Birmingham. His most outstanding legacy is his collection of photographs of which approximately 10,000 glass negatives are preserved in the Birmingham Central Library.